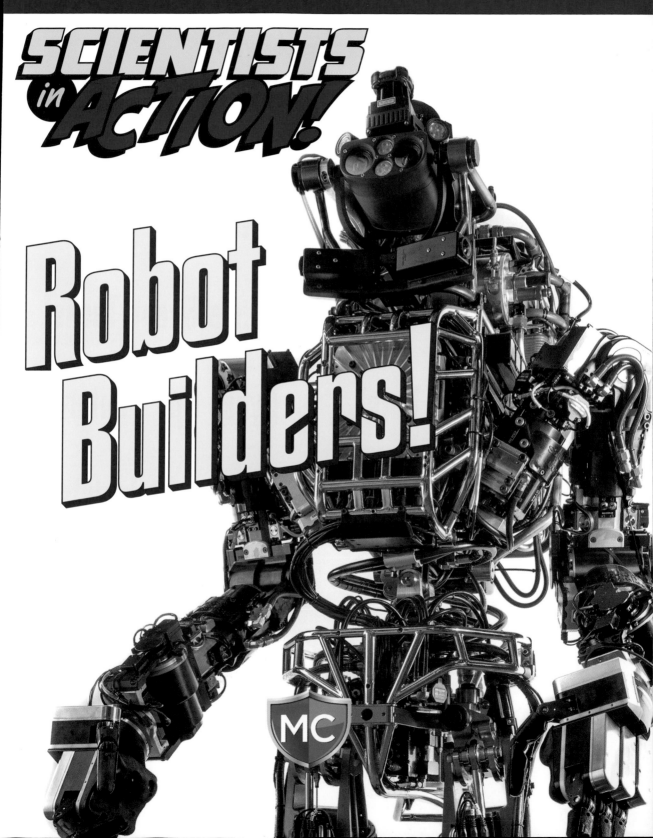

CREATE THE FUTURE OF MACHINES WITH...

SCIENTISTS in ACTION!

Robot Builders!

Archaeologists!

Astronauts!

Big-Animal Vets!

Biomedical Engineers!

Civil Engineers!

Climatologists!

Crime Scene Techs!

Cyber Spy Hunters!

Marine Biologists!

Robot Builders!

Scientists in Action!

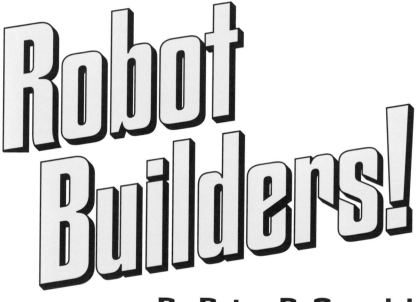

Robot Builders!

By Betsy R. Cassriel

Mason Crest
450 Parkway Drive, Suite D
Broomall, PA 19008
www.masoncrest.com

© 2016 by Mason Crest, an imprint of National Highlights, Inc.

Printed and bound in the United States of America.

Series ISBN: ISBN: 978-1-4222-3416-7
Hardback ISBN: 978-1-4222-3426-6
EBook ISBN: 978-1-4222-8487-2

First printing
1 3 5 7 9 8 6 4 2

Produced by Shoreline Publishing Group LLC
Santa Barbara, California
Editorial Director: James Buckley Jr.
Designer: Tom Carling, Carling Design Inc.
Production: Sandy Gordon
www.shorelinepublishing.com
Cover image: DARPA

Library of Congress Cataloging-in-Publication Data

Cassriel, Betsy, author.
    Robot builders! / by Betsy R. Cassriel.
    pages cm. -- (Scientists in action!)
    Audience: Grades 9 to 12
Includes bibliographical references and index.
ISBN 978-1-4222-3426-6 (hardback : alk. paper) -- ISBN 978-1-4222-3416-7 (series : alk. paper) -- ISBN 978-1-4222-8487-2 (ebook) 1. Robots--Juvenile literature. 2. Robotics--Juvenile literature. I. Title.
TJ211.2.C37 2016
629.8'92--dc23
                2015004816

Contents

Key Icons to Look For

Words to Understand: These words with their easy-to-understand definitions will increase the reader's understanding of the text, while building vocabulary skills.

Sidebars: This boxed material within the main text allows readers to build knowledge, gain insights, explore possibilities, and broaden their perspectives by weaving together additional information to provide realistic and holistic perspectives.

Research Projects: Readers are pointed toward areas of further inquiry connected to each chapter. Suggestions are provided for projects that encourage deeper research and analysis.

Text-Dependent Questions: These questions send the reader back to the text for more careful attention to the evidence presented here.

Series Glossary of Key Terms: This back-of-the-book glossary contains terminology used throughout this series. Words found here increase the reader's ability to read and comprehend higher-level books and articles in this field.

WORDS TO UNDERSTAND

collaborates   works together, as on a team or
in a group

detect   uncover or discover by means of searching
for clues or evidence

humanoid   a machine designed to look like a human
being

meltdown   in a nuclear reactor, when the core gets so
hot that it melts through its container

rubble   the fragmented remains of a building after a
disaster or destruction

Action!

Mission Impossible?

It is 2 A.M. Dr. Dennis Hong pours himself another cup of coffee. He and his team are working hard in the Robotics and Mechanisms Lab (RoMeLa). Their mission: to develop a humanoid rescue robot. This robot has to go where men dare not go. The robot has to enter a building damaged by a natural disaster such as an earthquake or tsunami. It has to climb over **rubble** and move obstacles in its path. The usual wheels and treads are not going to work. It needs to be like a human with feet and legs that can climb. Not only that, the robot also has to detect any toxic leaks, locate a shut-off value, and stop the leak. This is the most difficult mission Hong has faced, but as he works into the night, he is positive that he and his team can take it on!

Robots don't really eat ice cream, of course, but Dr. Hong's robot-building team is working on ways to make robots more and more like people.

This mission is just one of many challenges Dennis Hong faces. He is a robot scientist born in California and raised in Seoul, South Korea. When Hong was six years old, he saw the movie *Star Wars*. He was amazed by the robots. In *Perspective*, a journal published by the University of Wisconsin-Madison College of Engineering, Hong said, "I still cannot forget the mind-blowing sensation when I first watched the movie *Star Wars*. I was fascinated by R2-D2 and C-3PO. Since then, I decided to become a robot scientist and never changed my mind...It might sound crazy, but that movie completely changed my life."

When Hong was a child, he spent a lot of time building things—and breaking them! With his brother and sister he made firecrackers and gunpowder. One day, they used the gunpowder to launch a rocket off the roof of their high-rise apartment building. The flame from the ignited gunpowder rose 15 feet (4.6 m) high. The security guards were angry, but their father was not. Hong's father was an aerospace engineer who led South Korea's short-range missile program. He approved of his children's experimenting.

After finishing high school in Korea, Hong went to the University of Wisconsin-Madison to study mechanical engineering. When he started college in the United States after living in Korea, it was hard at first. Gradually, he adjusted to a new life and a new culture. Next, Hong went to Purdue University in Indiana to complete a master's and doctorate degree. Today, Hong is an assistant professor of mechanical engineering at Virginia Polytechnic Institute. He also established and is in charge of the Robotics and Mechanisms Lab (RoMeLa). He teaches classes and works with teams of students on robotics projects. Hong loves what he does.

Tonight in the RoMeLa lab, the lights are blazing, and Hong glances over to see one of his students finishing a cup of coffee. Yes, it is late—again, Hong thinks. He works very long hours in the lab with his team of computer software and mechanical engineering students from the university. Every day, Hong inspires his students to improve the world with robotics. Two years ago, they worked on an automatic car for people with poor sight to drive. His team **collaborates** on these projects with teams from other universities and companies.

Hong looks over the shoulder of one of his computer engineers as she punches code into the computer. This week, the team has been working on its **humanoid** robot's balance. The robot walks on two legs

DARPA Challenges

The annual DARPA challenge creates a series of tests for robots. The robot builders have to design their robot to be as accomplished as possible. The robot that scores the highest on the difficult test is the winner, and can earn the creators a large government contract for more research. Here are some of the tasks that robots have faced in the challenges:

- get in a Jeep
- drive to a building
- exit the Jeep
- move obstacles
- open a door
- **detect** a toxic leak
- find the shut-off valve and turn it off
- climb a ladder
- walk across a narrow walkway
- use a power tool

like a human, and the team is trying to copy how a person's leg muscles work. Each time its robot walks across uneven ground in a test, it falls over! This week, the team has been working out how the robot's hand will grip the power tool while its thumb switches on the power. Each time they test it, the power tool falls out of the robotic hand.

The rescue robot mission they are working on is actually a competition. The competition is organized and funded by DARPA, or Defense Advanced Research Projects Agency, in response to the huge earthquake and tsunami that rocked Japan in 2011. Along with billions of dollars of damage, the earthquake and tsunami caused the Fukushima Nuclear Plant to begin a **meltdown**. This was very serious and very dangerous. People could not enter the nuclear plant to control the meltdown. After this terrible situation, the United States Department of Defense wanted engineers to work on robots as a solution to hazardous situations like that one.

When DARPA announced the rescue robot competition, Dr. Hong jumped at the chance. He loves that kind of challenge. When he was interviewed about it in *Virginia Tech News,* he said, "This is the craziest, boldest, most expensive, most challenging, yet possibly the most important robotics project in the history of mankind. We have a mission. Whether we succeed or not, if the technology we develop through this project can even save a single person's life in the future, then everything is worth it. We believe we are truly changing the world. This challenge was probably what I was born for."

One of the robots from Hong's lab is designed to move like a snake as it climbs this pole.

In the lab, the team gathers around the robot, watching it climb clumsily up a step. After many adjustments in the software coding, the robot climbs up the step without falling. Success! With a lot of cheering and high fives, Hong and his students head home for some needed sleep. They will be up early tomorrow working again. Winning any part of the competition will mean prize money for the RoMeLa lab and a lot of attention from other robotics professionals and the press! It also means that the team can contribute its knowledge and experience to the growing field of robotics.

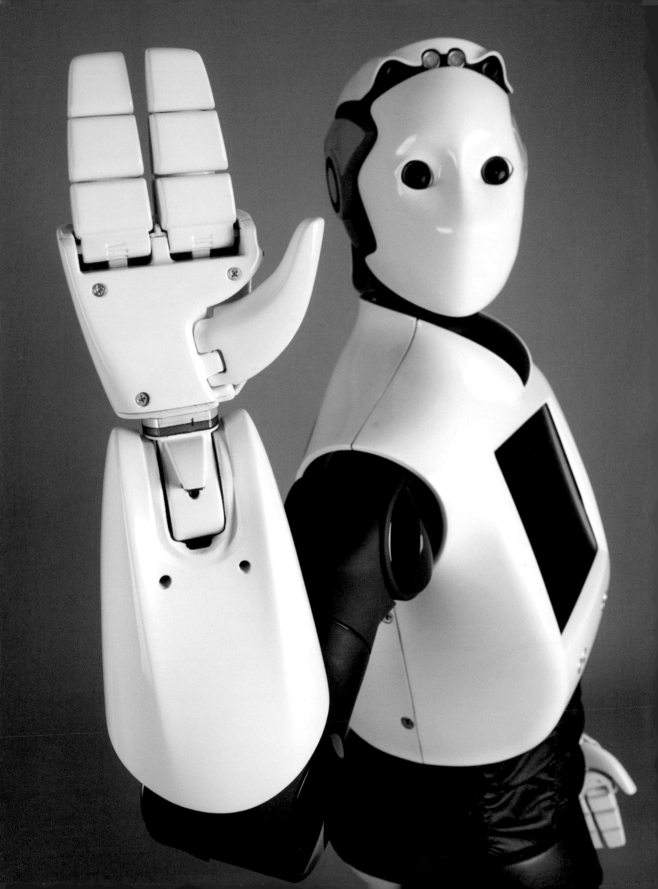

The Scientists and Their Science

To many people, the image of a robot is a powerful and evil humanoid like the Terminator of movie fame. In fact, a robot might look and talk like a human, but most do not. In fact, a robot is simply a machine that can do complex things that humans do. A robot may be **autonomous**, working on its own, or it may be controlled, moment-by-moment, by humans through computers or other controls. Through design and development, a robot engineer helps to make robots that can do tasks safely, easily, and efficiently.

WORDS TO UNDERSTAND

assembly lines   types of factory setups where parts are added one at a time to create a whole finished product

autonomous   able to work without direct human control

precise   very specifically measured to a tiny degree

roboticists   a term for robot scientists or engineers

trauma   a wound to the inside or outside of a body

Solving Real-Life Problems

*L*ike many scientists, robot scientists work to solve problems and to make life better for people. When a situation is dangerous, difficult, or dull for people, for example, scientists ask, "Can robotics help?" As they design, these engineers have to keep in mind not only the *how* but the *what*, *where*, and *who* of the robot. *What* are the robot's tasks and *where* will the robot have to do those tasks? Many robots will work outside the scientific laboratory with real people and everyday tools in tough environments. *Who* will be operating the robot? Depending on the application, people managing the robot could be highly skilled **roboticists**, workers in manufacturing plants, or soldiers in combat.

Engineers, then, work to develop many different kinds of robots. Many robots are used in manufacturing. For instance, scientists design robots that take the place of humans on production lines to manufacture cars and computers. Robots can do very **precise** work that is difficult for humans. A robot almost never makes a mistake, like a human might. Likewise, robots can move and manipulate heavy items. Industrial robots can also do the same job over and over again without getting fatigued or bored with the dull work. They do not ask for the day off, and they do not have trouble with their supervisors, either!

As with all robots, robot scientists have to be very careful in designing industrial robots. One important issue is safety. Humans have to be able to work safely around the robots. Flexibility is also a goal. Many industrial robots are simply robotic arms doing the same task again and again, but engineers want to see flexible robots that do multiple tasks alongside humans.

Industrial robots such as Baxter can be programmed to do just about anything on an assembly line. They can perform the same task over and over again, without mistakes and without getting tired.

Baxter, a robot developed by Rethink Robotics, can be programmed to do many different jobs such as packaging products or moving objects along **assembly lines**. Rethink engineers have made Baxter simple to use—like using a tablet! In the future we will see many more robots like Baxter working in factories.

In the United States, much of the funding for very innovative robotics development comes from the military—and this is where the action is. With funding from the government, scientists look at solutions that can protect police officers, firefighters, rescue workers, and soldiers in dangerous situations. Since fire is a serious danger, engineers are working on applying robotics technology to fire fighting.

SAFFIR, or Shipboard Autonomous Fire Fighting Robot, is a humanoid robot built at the Naval Research Laboratory to fight fires on ships. SAFFIR has been designed to maintain good balance on a rocking ship in the ocean. It uses sensors to avoid obstacles in its way and to throw "grenades" of fire-extinguishing chemicals.

In what other ways can robots help soldiers? Engineers at Boston Dynamics developed BigDog to help soldiers carry heavy loads. BigDog

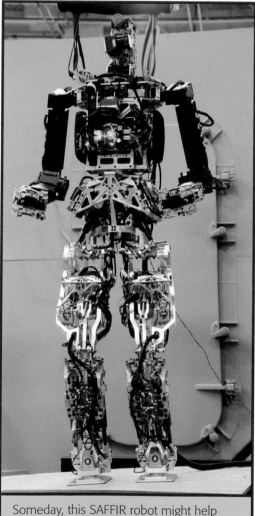

Someday, this SAFFIR robot might help save lives fighting fires on ships.

is a big robot with four legs that can carry heavy things over rough terrain. It can run, walk, and catch its balance if pushed. Operation is simple. A soldier controls BigDog with a smartpad on his or her wrist. BigDog will even follow along behind the operator like a dog with its owner. Helping ground soldiers manage their heavy equipment is an important use for robots.

Scientists are also working on tiny flying spies. DARPA wants a "perch-and-stare" micro air vehicle that can fly to a difficult target, land and perch nearby, do surveillance, and return to home base. U.S. and European armed forces already use small unmanned aircraft systems (UAS) like these. They fit into a backpack and are launched by being thrown by hand into the air.

Brave New Worlds

Scientists are working on using robotics in space and for under-sea exploration. For example, as you read this, the robot rover *Curiosity* is crawling across the surface of Mars, its instruments sending information back to scientists on Earth. *Curiosity* is one of the most complex robots in the world, and creates new visions of Mars every day of its mission.

Dextre, an astronaut-robot, is doing important work in space right now. Created by Canadian scientists, Dextre is a "handyman" robot with many arms. It is attached to the International Space Station (ISS) and can replace outside parts and move objects on the space station as well as guide astronauts on space walks. Astronauts control Dextre from inside the space station with joysticks. Meanwhile, on board ISS, the humanoid Robonaut is on duty to help monitor systems on the station and help with experiments.

In addition to the seemingly endless world of space, scientists have a lot to learn about worlds under the sea. Much of Earth's surface is covered with water, and roboticists are designing robots to help marine biologists, geologists, and others explore these deep places. Some of the underwater robots are remote-controlled vehicles, while others are very small submarines with a human crew and robotic arms. Still others, such as Autosub, created in the United Kingdom, are autonomous. Autosub can navigate to a certain point and carry out experiments with video, sonar, and other technologies. Autosub has performed many missions such as locating important metals on a lake floor and diving beneath the ice of Antarctica. Places like these in sea and space are the "last frontiers" of scientific exploration.

Dr. Robot?

A very exciting area of application for robots is in the field of medicine. Scientists are designing tiny robotic tools for surgery. The DaVinci is one robot used by doctors in operations such as heart surgery. By using a system like this for surgery, there is less scarring, **trauma**, and recovery time for the patient. That's because very small incisions are made for the tools to enter the patient's body at the surgical site. The surgeon sits at a console and sees a magnified 3-D image of the surgical site on the computer screen. As the surgeon works at the console controlling the surgical instruments, he or she can see the movements of the tools precisely. One surgeon at the Robotic Surgery Center at NYU's Langone Medical Center said, "It's as if I've miniaturized my body and gone inside the patient."

Becoming a Robot Engineer

How do you get a job working with robots? The first step is to take high school science, math, computer science, and applied technology courses. After that, you will be ready to study engineering in college. In some areas, colleges have programs in which students can earn a technical certificate to be a robotics technician. Many technicians work in manufacturing plants installing, operating, and maintaining robots and their systems.

Other roboticists research, design, develop, and test robots. Those scientists have a bachelor's degree in engineering. They may also earn a professional engineer (PE) certification by completing a bachelor's degree in engineering, getting work experience, and passing two professional exams. Many engineers who research and design robots have a master's degree or a Ph.D., too. They work in laboratories at universities, government organizations, and engineering companies.

Robot engineers are naturally creative problem solvers who are both self-motivated and self-directed. They like to analyze details and

The work of robot engineers can end up in space. Here, NASA scientists work on parts for the robotic rovers that were sent to explore Mars and send back information via satellite.

A Job to Love

Here is what Paulo Younse, a young mechanical engineer at the Jet Propulsion Lab (JPL) in Pasadena, California, said on Imagiverse.com about his job as a robot engineer: "I LOVE my job at JPL, where I get to design, build, and test robots. I get to use nearly everything I learned in school to do my job, and there are always new challenges involved where I continuously get to read and learn even more. I also get to work with a lot of very smart, creative, and exciting people who are willing to teach me what they know and work with me on different projects. Most of all, I love getting the chance to come up with new ideas for how to explore space, the solar system, and beyond."

think critically. They ask a lot of questions and do a lot of experimenting. They fail a lot, but when they fail, they see it as an opportunity to learn. Their motto, of course, is "try, try again."

Physically, robot engineers need good close-up vision and finger dexterity. They need a lot of energy and enthusiasm, too. They may have to sacrifice free time working long hours to meet deadlines or solve urgent problems. Engineering work environments are often casual, and people wear casual clothes—except if they are working in a "clean room" in which no dust can enter. They are careful to follow the strict safety rules of their lab or company to keep everyone from danger.

Engineers love being part of a team. They know they need an entire team of computer scientists, mechanical engineers, and more to be successful. They have good communication and "people skills." As part of their everyday work, they do a great deal of training, writing reports, and presenting ideas. Communicating well with others is at the heart of the job.

Text-Dependent Questions

1. What is the definition of a robot?

2. Name two robots from this chapter and how they are used.

3. What two different types of jobs for robot engineers are described here?

Research Project

What kind of robot would be helpful to you and your friends or family? What would it do? What would it look like? Design a robot and write a description of what it does. Then share your design ideas.

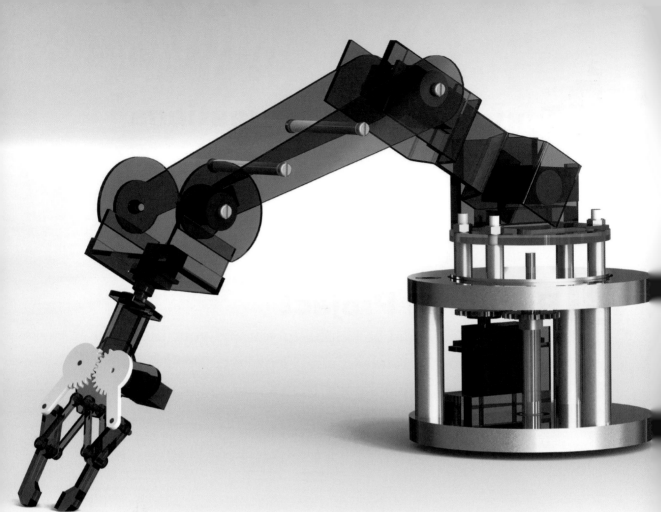

WORDS TO UNDERSTAND

3-D printer a machine that produces three-dimensional objects by layering plastic or other material

budget a set amount of money set aside for a particular purpose

prototypes first or preliminary models of something, especially a machine

soldering a process of using melted metal to connect objects to each other

Tools of the Trade

The results of the work of robot engineers are some of the most amazing and coolest machines in the world. To do that work, the engineers need some of the most high-tech tools and gear around. However, making a robot also means mastering some low-tech operations.

Software

The first steps in most robots' design start in a computer. After determining what the goal of the robot's movements will be, scientists sketch out ways to accomplish their task. Most use computer-aided design (CAD) software. Such programs let the user try out many different designs, then look at those designs from many angles. The computer also helps the designer make measurements, create objects in the right scale, and even estimate the weight of parts.

Computers are also essential to robot engineers because computer software makes robots move and "think." Each robot needs to be programmed to understand its job and its tasks. Robot scientists are often expert programmers who can write the language and code needed to tell their robots what to do. Even if they do not do the code themselves, engineers have to understand what that code or computer language can do so they can create a robot that can actually work!

The code is fed into the robot's systems by circuit boards and wiring, though many robots now work wirelessly. They receive messages from a tablet or smartphone, then perform their missions. Whether it is working on a preprogrammed circuit or changes its movements based on commands or information it gathers itself, nearly every robot depends on computers of one sort or another.

Hardware

Robots are machines, and machines can be made of just about any material. As they construct robots, robot engineers need hardware such as metals, plastics, foam, springs, gears, belts, wheels, and more to build the body of a robot. Each robot calls for a different shape or a different body. A robot that will work in water needs its insides to be waterproof. A robot that will work outside needs a tough outer shell to protect it. Engineers choose the materials for their robots based on the needs of the project . . . and the **budget** they have to work under!

In order to put all those pieces of material together, robot engineers get out their tools. While high-end computers are used to make the "brain" of the robot, making the bodies calls for smart work with hand tools. Robot engineering shops have drills, welding torches, and

Before a robot can be put through its paces, it goes through testing in a lab. Robot engineers need to have skills working with hand tools and power tools to make sure the robot is ready to go to work.

metal-cutting machines. It's like an industrial machine shop, with wrenches, **soldering** irons, and screwdrivers. Engineers choose nuts, bolts, wires, or clamps to hold pieces together. Depending on the robot's needs, the builders might include a radio receiver/transmitter, metal arms or hands, or even tablets to let people interact with the robot.

One key step is getting power to the robot. To make these machines go, engineers choose a power source that works best for the robot's environment and task. Batteries are the most common form of power. They come in many sizes and types, and some can be recharged to keep the robot going. The batteries provide power to the motors and gears that make the parts of the robot move.

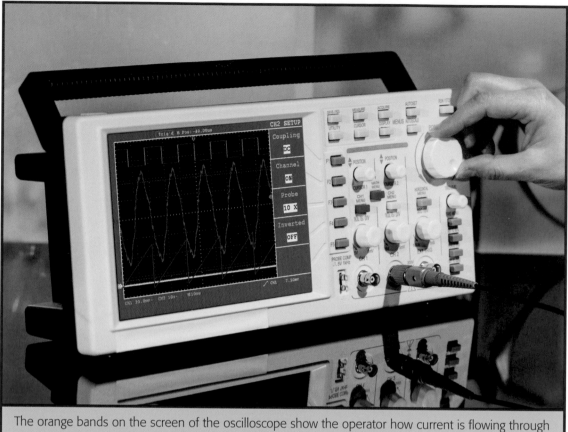

The orange bands on the screen of the oscilloscope show the operator how current is flowing through the machine or robot that is being worked on. The operator can adjust the dials for the best flow.

To make sure all these electronics and software are working, scientists have a variety of measuring tools. An oscilloscope looks like a small television set with a graph on the screen. The graph shows how the electrical signal of voltage changes over time. Oscilloscopes are used by a huge range of scientists, including robot engineers, for designing and repairing electronic equipment. The Digital Multi Meter (DMM), which gives information about electrical circuits, is another tool used by roboticists. A DMM is used to solve electrical problems and to test electrical repairs. A basic DMM measures resistance, voltage, and continuity. It is used to test batteries, measure a circuit's capacity, or find an electrical short. It is used in robotics and any other field using electrical work.

Reading the World

*M*any robots that are built from hardware and run by software need to have "senses," too. Special pieces of gear called sensors provide that information to the robot. Sensors gather information from the environment around the robot and translate that into digital signals that the machine can read. Just as your eyes and ears help you, sensors help a robot see and hear. Cameras, audio receivers, and microphones are part of many robots. They give a robot the ability to sense itself and the world around it.

Laser scanners help a robot detect obstacles in its path. A laser light shoots out ahead of the robot. When the beam hits an object, the robot can know to move around it or over it. Bar code readers, as used in

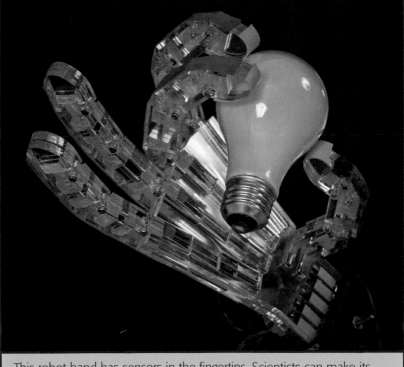

This robot hand has sensors in the fingertips. Scientists can make its touch so gentle that it can pick up a glass light bulb without breaking it.

stores, lets robots identify objects and locations. Sensors can also be placed in a humanoid robot's fingers to help it "feel" objects based on their shape and surface materials.

Where They Work

Most robot engineers are employed in offices, manufacturing plants, or laboratories. Typically, robot engineers split their time between office and lab. In the office, they are writing reports and working on plans. In the lab, they work on all different components of their robots. You will find most robots in the automotive industry, on vehicle assembly lines. However, engineers and their robots also work in the food-packaging, appliance-building, and electronic industries.

3-D Printers

Making the thousands of small parts that go into a robot can be a challenging task. It especially can be hard if you are designing new parts and want to see how they work. An emerging technology is making that work easier for roboticists. A **3-D printer** forms an object out of plastic or similar material. It is much like a laser printer that puts words or pictures on a piece of paper, but the 3-D printer creates three-dimensional physical objects. Engineers and designers use 3-D printing to make **prototypes** and test products. A prototype is a model of something, especially a machine, from which other forms are developed. Engineers can quickly make real-world prototypes this way.

Clean Room

Before the robot rover *Curiosity* reached Mars, it had to be built. It was built in one of the cleanest environments on earth. In a "clean room," the level of contamination—such as dust, airborne microbes, aerosol particles, and chemical vapors—is controlled with air filters. Even the tiniest of those things could damage the sensitive gear in the rover, making

Safety Equipment

Engineers are careful to stay safe as they work. Equipment such as safety glasses, goggles, face shields, and gloves are important because they protect the eyes and skin from chips, sparks, or dust that tools and other equipment can create. If dust, fumes, or mists are produced, a scientist also needs to wear a respirator. When working with noisy motors or power tools, engineers protect their hearing with earphones. In some jobs, engineers wear lab coats or other uniforms.

it break down or not work. For the engineers, however, actually keeping a clean room completely clean can be hard work.

"Humans are the dirtiest things to enter a clean room," said Victor Mora, a supervisor at NASA, so scientists working in a clean room have to "come clean" themselves. They take an air shower, which is like a regular shower but instead of water, they are blasted with air. It removes contaminants from clothing.

Scientists also enter and exit through an air lock, which is a very small "room" with airtight doors on either side. The doors can't be opened at the same time. A scientist enters through one door, which closes behind him. He is in a small room with doors at the front and the back. Then the door in front opens. In this way the contaminated air outside cannot get inside the lab. A scientist working in a clean room also wears a special "bunny suit" with a hood, face mask, gloves, boots, and coveralls. They also clean their hands and face before they put on the protective gear.

This robot is designed to move like a horse. It can carry hundreds of pounds of gear for soldiers in the field. They operate the robot with remote control.

Finding Ideas

Scientists get ideas from things they see in real life. They study how people and animals move, and they try to use those movements in their designs. It is called "biomimicry." For example, Dennis Hong from Virginia Tech watched a mother braid her daughter's hair. After that, he designed a three-legged walking machine that moved with the same kind of braiding motion. On another day, he thought about how a cowboy lassos a horse. Based on that, he designed a robot that wraps around a pole or table like a rope.

Many robots today use wheels and treads to move, but in nature there are no wheels or treads. Animals and insects crawl, run, fly, walk, jump, and slither. One group of robot engineers in Japan designed a robot after studying the movement of snakes. The bot is small and "slithers" in small places where human rescuers can't reach. Other scientists are studying beetles, grasshoppers, spiders, bees, and dogs as they build robots. When scientists get ideas from nature or biology, it is called "bioinspiration." A team at Portsmouth University in England designed Robobug after looking at crabs and spiders. Robobug has eight legs and can climb up walls and across ceilings. It can also carry twice its own weight.

Text-Dependent Questions

1. What kinds of technology are used for robots' artificial intelligence?

2. What is the name of a lab where contamination such as dust is carefully controlled?

3. What is "bioinspiration"?

Research Project

Search on the Internet under "biomimicry." Learn how engineers have used biomimicry in their designs. Write a short report to share with others.

Tales From the Field!

World Cup 2050: Seeing Glory

Can robots play soccer? RoboCup is an annual soccer tournament for robots, and some robot engineers' goal is to create a robot soccer team that can beat the human World Cup champions by 2050. Designing a robot that can find and kick a soccer ball and go around other players is a real challenge. Robot scientists take this challenge because the technology they develop can be used by other scientists—and because it's fun!

WORDS TO UNDERSTAND

exoskeletons   mobile machines with an outer framework worn by a person to give power and energy to the arms and legs

nanobots   robots that are so small they can only be seen with microscopes

prostheses   artificial limbs built to replace missing limbs on people

simulation   a program that copies or mimics a real-life situation

There are five different Robocup leagues. The **Simulation** League plays in a virtual soccer stadium and is run by autonomous software programs. The small and medium leagues use small robots that do not look like humans and are controlled by a team of people on computers next to the field. The Standard Platform league uses small humanoid robots. Amazingly, these robots play soccer autonomously without outside human control.

Finally, the Humanoid League has people-sized robots. Soccer-playing robots have to run, change direction, jump, and kick. Balance is a tough problem for designers to solve. Each of the Standard Platform Robocup bots has a gyroscope to help it react to change of direction and balance. Each has 25 joints in its arms, fingers, legs, neck, back, and hips. Moreover, it has two cameras in its head and sensors in its chest and feet to measure distance and contact with the ball.

So far, the robots are awkward and slow, but scientists such as Dennis Hong are seeking victory in this league. When Professor Hong first glimpsed the coveted Louis Vuitton Humanoid Cup, he gazed at the trophy and promised his students, "We're going to bring it home."

Amazon's Robot Army

Amazon is the biggest online superstore, and its customers want their purchases delivered now. Filling millions of orders and shipping out packages is a real challenge, so a few years ago Amazon bought Kiva Systems, a Massachusetts company that makes warehouse robots and software. Today, Amazon uses 15,000 different robots to work with packages in its warehouses.

Small orange robots move throughout the warehouse by reading signals from an invisible grid. They can find everything from vitamins

This flying robot used by Amazon could someday carry packages from warehouses directly to people's homes. It might use GPS to track its location. The package is in the orange box at the bottom.

to smartphones to stuffed animals. Warehouse workers used to walk 10 to 12 miles a day. Now robots bring an entire stack of shelves to the workers. The robots can lift up to 750 pounds and have motion sensors to stop them from running into anything. What used to take an hour and a half to get shipped now may take only 15 minutes.

So far, the robots do the easy part of moving things around the warehouse. People do the complicated part of making sure the right product gets to the right customer. Amazon, however, is already working on the next thing: an unmanned flying drone that can deliver packages to customers' homes. These drones, called "Octocopters," can carry a package of up to five pounds and have a built-in GPS to find customers' houses. The drone is electric and autonomous. It's still being tested, but might one day make its way to your door.

The Bionic Man

Hugh Herr is a bionic man. He is also a double amputee. In 1982, when he was a star of the rock-climbing world, Herr lost both his legs to frostbite in a mountaineering expedition. Today, he is head of the biomechatronics group at Massachusetts Institute of Technology's Media Lab.

Hugh Herr combined his expertise in robotics with his need for replacement limbs to help many people walk again.

In general, most **prostheses** might look like a leg and foot, but they don't work like a leg and foot. In fact, they can be awkward and often painful. So, for many years Herr and his crew in the lab have been working on making better prostheses and **exoskeletons**. Today they have replaced the action of leg muscles with technology. With new technologies like small microprocessors, sensing capabilities, power supplies, and motors, Herr's group has developed PowerFoot BiOM.

PowerFoot BiOM is the first lower-leg system to use robotics to replace what muscles and tendons do in a leg, ankle, and foot. PowerFoot BiOM is a computerized ankle–foot system that actually propels the user forward with each step. Incredibly, it measures the angle and speed as the heel of the foot hits the ground. Then it uses its computer to respond with the speed and angle for a comfortable next step.

Herr said, "We are constantly surrounded by messages about how technology is not doing us well: pollution and nuclear weapons and so on. I'm an example of the opposite trend." Herr wants to use science and technology to make both disabled and nondisabled people better, stronger, faster.

Really Tiny Robots

Scientists hope that tiny robots can be put inside people to do jobs that can't be done with surgery or help ease the harsh side effects

Wearable Robotics

Move over Iron Man and Avatar—this is not the movies anymore. Scientists are developing exoskeletons that give people superhuman powers. By using an exoskeleton (below), a soldier can carry heavy gear over long distances without getting tired, or rescue wounded soldiers from the battlefield easily. However, superpowers might be available to "regular people" soon as well. One exoskeleton developed by Harvard, called the "Soft Exosuit," is comfortable and made of fabric. When a person wears it when walking, it gives power to the muscles to provide more stamina, strength, and balance.

This is just an artist's drawing, but the idea is real: Super-tiny robots that can work inside a person's body.

caused by treatments such as chemotherapy. Scientists at Chonnam National University in South Korea have developed a microscopic robot that can detect and treat cancer from inside the body. This amazing area of robotics is a form of nanotechnology, and these miniscule **nanobots** are called "bacteriobots." It works like this: Bacteria is attached to a tiny artificial body that can travel through the human body. These bacteria are attracted to substances found near cancer cells. When this little bot finds cancer cells, it sprays them with anticancer drugs. As of 2015, the bacteriobots have been tested on mice. It will be some time before they are tested on humans, but the possibilities are inspiring.

Asimo, Rock Star of Robots

*I*n 2014, the most famous robot in the world met one of the most important people in the world. Created by the Honda Corporation in Japan, Asimo is one of the most advanced humanoid robots ever made. Roboticists at Honda have been working on Asimo since 1986. Asimo is like a child "growing up" over time. The roboticists who work on Asimo dream that robots will coexist with humans. They want to design robots to help people and ask, "What kind of robot can change society, make people happy, and make life easier?"

At a meeting in Japan, Asimo met President Barack Obama. First, two cameras in Asimo's face used facial recognition technology to help the robot identify the president from among a group of people.

Asimo, from Honda, has been programmed to take part in demonstrations. The robot shows off its abilities to walk, carry things, communicate, and even run. It's one of the few robots that can do that.

Then Asimo walked up to the president and welcomed him. The president seemed impressed when Asimo said to him, "I can run really fast. Let me show you," and ran across the floor. A major issue in designing a robot to run and jump is balance. When a person runs, both feet leave the ground for a second. The Honda team designed Asimo to lean forward, back, and side-to-side to stay balanced as he moves.

Finally, to finish off the meeting, Asimo identified the president in the crowd again and told him, "I can kick a soccer ball, too." After telling the president that he would kick the ball right to him, Asimo sent the soccer ball straight to President Obama, who stopped it with his foot. Another small step forward for robotkind…

FIRST Robotics Competition

"*I*n high school, I began looking forward to taking part in FIRST as soon as I started at the academy," explained Yesenia, a student from Santa Barbara (California) Dos Pueblos Engineering Academy. FIRST stands for "For Inspiration and Recognition of Science and Technology." When Yesenia walked into the school shop with all its tools and machines for the first time, she was thrilled. The students had to do everything themselves. They started by making models with wood, aluminum, steel, wire, and soldering. They also needed to do mechanical and computer-assisted design.

FIRST works to foster an interest in Science, Technology, Engineering, and Mathematics (STEM) education, which includes events such as their FIRST Robotics Competition. In the FIRST Robotics Competition, students work with mentors and community sponsors to design and build a robot that will compete against other FIRST teams in a specific mission during regional and national events.

Students from the Dos Pueblos Engineering Academy work on their robot during a FIRST competition. Working with mentors and teachers, they do all the work needed to design and build the robot.

Many months later, after developing their robot, Yesenia and her teammates walked into the competition arena. Their moment had come. The team's robot was ready. Everything that the team had been working on had paid off. The robot performed well. The team won that event in California! The team members earned medals and the cheers of the crowd at the arena where the event was held. The feeling of pride and accomplishment is something they will never forget!

Robot engineers of all ages are working around the world to use technology to help people and explore the planet. They are adding every day to the fields they impact with their work. Today, they are working in the medical field, in space, in the military, and in laboratories and factories. Tomorrow, they might hit hit the road to create vehicles, build home-based robots that create free time for human beings, or design robots that can entertain or even teach.

Young people of all ages and interests can find something in robotics to enjoy. The future of robotics needs creative, energetic, and enthusiastic people to help take giant steps forward.

The work takes scientific knowledge and technical skill, but the one thing that unites robot builders is that they are all dreamers. They ask the questions "What if…" and "Why not?" and then use their imagination and skill to make their dreams come true.

 Text-Dependent Questions

1. What is helping Amazon ship products faster?
2. What "missions" did Asimo have when he met President Obama, and did he accomplish his missions?
3. Who participates in FIRST Robotics Competition?

Research Project

What is your favorite robot movie? Watch the movie and write about the robot's special abilities and how these abilities help or hurt people.

Scientists in the News

Making a Robot Friend

Cynthia Breazeal has always imagined robots with emotions and feelings. When she was in third grade, she wrote a story about a robot with emotions that ran on a computer. Today, Dr. Cynthia Breazeal is director of the Personal Robots Group at the Massachusetts Institute of Technology. Breazeal wants to humanize technology so that a robot helps a person not just as a tool but also as a partner.

Breazeal is developing a small robot named Jibo, a social robot for the home. She imagines Jibo having a "role" in a family just like any other member does. Jibo reminds people of their schedules, takes photos of them, relays texts and voicemails, and even reads stories to children.

To build Jibo, Breazeal used crowdfunding, a way to raise money from a large number of people on the Internet. She raised money by pre-selling Jibos to donors.

Unlike mobile phones and com-

Say hello to Jibo, an in-home robot.

puters that do some similar things as Jibo, Jibo interacts socially with people and shows emotion. He is friendly, warm, and personal. He has two cameras to identify and track people, microphones that can locate sound, and touch sensors on his body. The biggest technical challenge Breazeal and her team face so far is integrating all of the information coming in from Jibo's sensors.

Robots on Camera

While scientists are working to make their imaginary robots into real machines, moviemakers are making imaginary robots "real," if only for the cameras. Steve Mahan works at the famous Hollywood special effects studio Legacy Effects. The studio worked on the Terminator movies with director James Cameron. For one scene in *Terminator 2*, he and his crew made 28 crushable robot skulls. Each time they shot the scene, something went wrong. Skull after skull was crushed. Finally, at the twenty-fifth skull, they got the shot to work.

Since that experience, Mahan has worked on character design and special effects for movies such as *Avatar, Iron Man, Aliens, Jurassic Park, Pearl Harbor,* and many more. He is not a scientist himself, but, like others in the entertainment industry, he consults and works with a full range of software, mechanical, electrical, and robot engineers to build animatronics.

Animatronics are robotic devices with the characteristics of animals or other creatures. They are used for film, theater, and theme parks. It takes a variety of people such as artists, sculptors, puppeteers, computer programmers, and engineers to design and build the characters. Through their work, we see better special effects in film each year.

Find Out More

Books

Buckley, James Jr. and Mark Shulman. *Time for Kids Explores Robots.* New York: Time Home Entertainment Inc., 2014.

Ceceri, Kathy. *Making Simple Robots: Exploring Cutting-Edge Robotics With Everyday Stuff.* Sebastapol, Calif.: Maker Media, 2015.

McComb, Gordon. *Arduino Robot Bonanza.* New York: McGraw-Hill/Tab Books, 2013.

Valk, Laurens. *LEGO Mindstorms EV3 Discovery Book: A Guide to Building and Programming Robots.* San Francisco: No Starch Press, 2014.

Web Sites

4-H Robotics (www.4-h.org)
Visit the national high school educational organization's site and search for "robotics." You'll find information about a program it runs to help teach basic robot science.

Science Buddies (www.sciencebuddies.org)
Search for "robotics engineer" and you'll be taken to several pages on this site about steps you can take to become a robot builder.

NASA and Robots (www.robotics.nasa.gov)
Find out how America's space agency is using robots in its missions, plus read how you can learn from NASA's experts.

Series Glossary of Key Terms

airlock   a room on a space station from which astronauts can move from inside to outside the station and back

anatomy   a branch of knowledge that deals with the structure of organisms

bionic   to be assisted by mechanical movements

carbon dioxide   a gas that is in the air that we breathe out

classified   kept secret from all but a few people in a government or an organization

deforestation   the destruction of forest or woodland

diagnose   to recognize by signs and symptoms

discipline   in science, this means a particular field of study

elite   the part or group having the highest quality or importance

genes   information stored in cells that determine a person's physical characteristics

geostationary   remaining in the same place above the Earth during an orbit

innovative   groundbreaking, original

inquisitiveness   an ability to be curious, to continue asking questions to learn more

internships   jobs often done for free by people in the early stages of study for a career

marine   having to do with the ocean

meteorologist   a scientist who forecasts weather and weather patterns

physicist   a scientist who studies physics, which examines how matter and energy move and relate

primate   a type of four-limbed mammal with a developed brain; includes humans, apes, and monkeys

traits   a particular quality or personality belonging to a person

Index

Photo Credits

RoMeLa: 6, 8, 11, 27; Reem Robotics: 12; Rethink Robotics: 15; U.S. Naval Research Lab/Jamie Hartman: 16; NASA: 19, 29; GrabCad.com: 22; Dreamstime.com: Luchschen 25, Andreus 38; DARPA: 30; Ralf Roletschek 32; Amazon: 35; Reel Abilities: 36; Raytheon: 37; Honda: 39; Dos Pueblos Engineering Academy: 41, 42; Jibo: 44.

Scientists in Action logo by Comicraft.

About the Author

Betsy R. Cassriel is a faculty member and department chair at Santa Barbara (California) City College. She has written three textbooks, including *Academic Connections 1* and *Stories Worth Reading 1 and 2*, for learners of English as a second language. She has a bachelor's degree in English from Westmont College and a master's degree in teaching from the School for International Training in Vermont. She lives in Santa Barbara with her family.